A Crawdad's Rhapsody

Poems By Fred Harrington

Rock
Ledge
Press

Photo credits:
  "Vistas," Smith family
  "Place," Smith family
  "Noise," Anne Shanahan
  Cover, Getty iStock
  About the Author, Mary Harrington

Poems previously published:
"Somnolent," Lake Country Echo, Conesus, New York
"Not Until After," Garbanzo Volume Five, Seraphemera Books, Bethel, Connecticut/Houston, Texas

Edited by: Jacqueline.wordsmith
Cover design: Rock Ledge Press

Rock
Ledge
Press

Published by Rock Ledge Press, Bethel, CT 06801
Printed in the U.S.A.

A Crawdad's Rhapsody

Poems of various sensibilities,
including haikus and a senryu

By Fred Harrington

(Known to his college friends as Crawdad)

WENDY

NEVER STOP BEING SURPRISED

THIS — ANOTHER

BIG LOVE,

Sm

Foreword

The author, left, and long-time friend Jim Smith at Canandaigua Lake, a Finger Lake in upstate New York.

Vistas

A photo — from many decades past.
It speaks to most of both their lives,
measured as days are often tallied —
by the ways friendships mount up.

Some of their markers are minor
inconveniences of separations,
no matter the length — sufficiently
useful to gauge all the better ones.

Look closely.   Their eyes hold
reflections of a future that will
ultimately grow beyond the vistas
commonly considered tangible.

Sit quietly.   Watch.   Listen.
Their song holds universal truths
found in the joy of time together,
a trajectory for lives well-lived.

Their time, an invisible speck in
mankind's larger ledger includes
their varied pilgrimages across
paths made of words.

They sing to you now with some
kept sacred on the journey:
Friends, Family, Love & Place.
They invite you to sing along.

A Tanka for Mary

These words   a carpet
Our lives together   the ride
How long will it last
If gods know they will not say
So hold my hand   I love you

Contents

"There is this circle I walk
that I have learned to love."

~ *Jim Harrison, "In Search of Small Gods"*

This is

The First Part

Minimum Viewpoints

A black pre-dawn morning squeaks
twisted minimal reveille from every
cog as I open the vertical blinds.

Each vane now squared to the glass,
every space between them holds
its own long dark strip of out there.

Relationships revived in that
no-see-um world crawl away
from a rising sun.

A magnolia struggles to appear;
slower than Grammy opening
presents at Christmas.

The magnolia suggested becomes
itself below a sky's pastel promise,
minimum viewpoints expanding.

Each gaze brings all the more all.
Near noon it might be evidence.
By tonight, words stacked in bales.

Young Heart Old Heart

My young heart
was like a bird;
limited range
a hunger and
unreasoned need
in search of a
place to land.

My old heart,
more Voyager;
outbound,
time's lessons
      seeking more
with no interest
in landing.

Quilted Days

All are unique and precious,
made from the smoke of resolve,
the laughter on the wind of generations,
things known — turned with each telling.
Some may never be spoken of again.

Each day they are created adds yet
another of the patchwork quilt squares,
our moments passing decades to
this powerful cover taking shape.
The fabric colors dance.

A dark border notion would stifle
new rows and no trunk will ever be
used to contain this blanket which has
our lives as its stuffing.

In The Great Perhaps

It is a 1950 day today.
>I am a five-year-old boy lifting a Bakelite
receiver to mimic the operator repeating,
>>*"Number please."* Mother walks up quietly.
>>Takes it from my hand, whispers, *"Yes, I am
so very sorry. Yes, he is only four..."*

It is a 2018 day today.
>I am just another old guy sending phone
photos & messages to his son in upstate New
York. Both of us stand looking out windows; one
with two feet of snow, the other, where palms are
swaying.

It is today, today.
>I look out toward the palms, then down at my
phone with Tom's newest snowy news, then back
outside but my mind sees the dining room and my
mother, where it can remain 1950. It is one of the
multiplicities
>>I like to visit from time to time that I call
The Great Perhaps.

Acorns

I am now a seventy-plus child
just learning to walk. I can see
a huge floor model radio, and
hear a wolf howl. At The
Lone Ranger theme, I stumble
for the safety of Great-grandma
Brackett's knees in those flesh-
colored support hose, her wine-
colored Acorn slippers with
holes cut out for toes pointing
in unusual directions.

They always said I couldn't
possibly recall those days,
I was just a baby. They are all
dead and gone now as I see it
all once again, snuggled here
with my grandsons as I watch
them enjoy their *screen time,*
playing with those iPad things
as I scratch paper with a stick
of carbon and wiggle my toes
in my new gray Acorns.

Searching

The writing mounts up
for those bitten by the
magical bug whose
venom lasts a lifetime.

Journals grow from
a drawer full to a few
shelves worth and with
the birth of constant

new approaches and
inventive devices a
catalog of effort may
produce diamonds.

The trick for authors is
to continue digging into
their stacks of coal-like
struggles to find them.

Once in hand, the gems
must be sorted, placed
one after the other in a
catalogue.

This is place holder seven.

Spring

golden window sills

pine pollen wafting like clouds

life full of promise

No Poetic Wax 23

Walk with me through
yesterday's spaces
past the futures I rode
as other traces.
Take my hand; assurance
for the blank places
where old known paths
with too many new faces
keep me ghostly.

Has truth passed or the
past truth claimed
a seat for every table
that Temple Street house
ever filled on a Sunday's
worth of brunch or lunch?
The space seems greater than
a thought's worth of measure
from the porch at the Inn
to that one across the street.

Still, every god I have sought knows
the larger values I treasure.

Barbara Davis and Steph Smith at the Thinking Spot overlooking Cananadaigua Lake, land of the Seneca.

Place

This is the Other –
not the point where mendacity
has a seat at any table.
It is a locus of ritual,
of renewal and realigning.

It is a rare, precious speck
of the universe where
the glue is created for
putting new things together and
cementing pieces worth saving.

Here joining is beyond simplicity
of friendship, family and metaphor.
Your own dimming eyesight
witnesses the gaze of children
you treasure as your own.

And now in a twilight of moment or
something more, celebrate the magic
of blossoming possibilities and watch
them looking outward —
as we all must.

Another Photo

Captured lightning from a box in
her hand fastened a piece of our
life to an almost any time future
when you might see it again.

You do & don't get to choose.
You are twenty, seventy,
neither, both. It is the way
of most things.

You live, love, celebrate,
regret, don't, watch some,
understand little, look ahead,
behind, in between, don't.

Box lightning will always do
more than create moments. Each
piece of any past is impossible to
examine as hard as I stare.

Another photo.
Memory unleashed from a drawer.

Define III

the endured silence,
in a space without words
in a thought
or on paper.

＊＊＊

the greatest loved ones,
the depths of closest friendships
in those times
separated.

＊＊＊

the miles outward bound,
a cost incalculable
descending
to this mélange.

Firesign Choirboy

Amidst confusions,
one piled upon the next
things can strive for dominion
over *place.*

Adventure and fortune
with times gentle coaxing
may lead to the piece of a
truce withholding surrender.

I am forever a child of Temple Street
alone under a streetlamp's glow
standing in the night silence
with half-dollar snowflake company.

Grandson

There's a tug on the bay
convincing a barge to
see things its way.

There's a tug on my sleeve
coaxing my vision to
see so much more.

Flicker

The yellow-shafted flicker redefines persistence at a transition between snow and open grass under our pool deck where early afternoon sun warms his lunch on this glorious first day of a new year.

It prods, pokes, not moving along, remaining in one place, only one step now into the edge of the snow, burying its head while at its work until finally, another reward for the effort.

I will put these words away with their titled, tilted identity, silently giving thanks to all the small gods watching, for every opportunity the bird is granted as well as the blessings life passes my way.

An innate irony beyond words exists in this moment of watching a bird at its business. Time shimmers past all living things with each new day, each night, each choice made; each allotment.

Charade

She dressed as a scarecrow
sat in a lawn chair
bird seed in upright gloves
until they arrived daily
fooled by the charade.

Ever after she could put treats
in her bare hand — or yours
to reach out from inside the
back door or even outside
calling *chick-a-dee-dee-dee.*

In no time you would have them
perched on your hand.

May we all
do as much
so well.

In remembrance,
Doris Arlene Knitter Harrington

17

Define II

Nothing sits smiling,
a necessity;
holding tight to
his indecision ticket
on the turtle bus
because the last
fracture must heal
and after all …

Indecision works on
Her face too beside each unknown, the
unknown transfer
of question in
any size heart
too frightened in the
world full of thinking

on any bus
to anywhere.

Measure

measure your regrets

with a stick not used for the

scars you think you own

Creative Cussing

In my family, from the moment I began to learn our language, cussing was considered an art form.

To some on both sides but not to all of them.

Uncle Lee, Dad's youngest brother taught me cuss words very early, before I understood consequence.

Farm life: Grandma Ethel, a hard-core Baptist, encouraged me not to use cuss words, at least not so she would hear. The first time she heard one, she had been standing by the sink, invited me over, grabbed me in a head lock and choked me near to death with a bar of Fels-Naptha Soap, it has grit like Lava with that special naptha kick.

Like many things in a life, it was a memorable moment as well as an opportunity to shuffle attitudes about opportunities around while you grow up.

Brushing your teeth and having a clean mouth always meant something different from that day on.

Another Winter Wednesday

Backyard air fills with
sunlight sparkle, fine bits of
Icy snow slowly drifting past
another Wednesday noontime.

A hawk warns a crow away from
a pine hideout where it watches the
just-filled feeders below that may
help deliver its next warm meal.

The country quiet interrupted briefly
as a Big Beat teen junker thunders
down the road celebrating urgency
to be heard if not seen or understood.

Another winter Wednesday wonder
for reflections beyond any boundary
of sun on snow or survival for some
understandings past here at this now.

a haiku

Days before winter

snow knee-deep in the back yard

my leaf rake resting

Distinctions

I spook around inside the unlit
house looking out the windows
as dawn begins arriving.

In the earliest light of day, the deer
watch from the necessities out there
in the growing shadows they know.

We are a morning's
distinctions without
much difference.

Sandbox

At the kindergarten playground
one day after lunch, early in the
new world, I began to practice
personal exaggerations with
Mike Strother. I still exaggerate
him back into life, to be with me.

A local wizard froze me to a
paper moment standing next
to Joan Witherow. I went
home and told my mother I was
going to marry Joan.

I forgot by the next day before
it was time for lunch, I think
she said I love you about two
years later. So many words then
were so very brand new.
For all of us.

Now after fifty-plus years I hold
my Hopalong Cassidy lunch box,
stashed in the garage loft with
other *perfectly good* treasures
speculating if Mercury is in
retro-grade, wondering when
yesterday might jump way, way
beyond every tomorrow.

> I watch carefully.
> Listen intently
> For more words
> to use here:
> from this sandbox
> of a mind,
> outward-bound.

Late March

A late March sunrise

my hands full of Kerouac

my heart filled with friends

Aries horoscope: *In a world of speed, the one who takes time to do something that is right and beautiful down to the last detail will stand out. You're such a person today.*

The Last Detail

Stand out there in the world
where the edge speeds no faster
than the center

Perfection is always close
enough
Once you know it is there

Identity

Ghosts surrounded the spring
as moon shadows from nearby
trees darkened the path I took
toward the river.

One of them spoke:
You are many things. Too many things.
Some outside a reason for understanding,
a small piece from the creator's wish
in a time beyond knowledge, like words
spoken prior to definition.

You are earth from the valley of the Genesee,
its waters, nearby springs, creeks such as Oatka,
soot from our ancient fires, perfume of smoke
which whispered of your arrival from the other
side of the world.

***

I asked, Am I also a worn piece of paper that tells the
lies of my forbearers, bits of truths they believed and
the remnants of voices spoken to the people they
were unable to eradicate with finality?

I stepped cautiously, closer to the edge of the river.

A woman's gentle voice whispered,
Do you still keep the arrowhead
we left for you by the creek?

I answered with all the humility I could muster.
It is a great treasure. I have it in a special chest.

The moon and night sky began to give way to
the rising sun as I neared the water's edge,
listening until it was the color of the morning

Words With My Father

> I think of him often
> especially when
> I am shaving
> Two faces at once

Mother had handed me his Norelco
Here, shave your father
That one — a good day, the swelling
in his arm diminished in the midst
of the cancer that had closed his
throat. He was never the kind of
man to talk incessantly.

> Eyesight diminished
> I lean over the sink
> closer to the mirror
> His tongue tries to
> stretch his skin
> turning his face
> slightly

As if he is there I ask *Please don't.*
I can do that with my fingers.
My new two-tone Norelco buzzes
as the shorter whiskers are mowed
neatly away near my hand separating
my moustache

Arriving at Ghostly

You need no path to
arrive at ghostly.

Adjust and glide,
travel light
in quiet sounds
wander around
foggy apparition
for the right
time in the light
is not sorrow.

Give up on smoke debt
you can't borrow. Now
was always past with
distinctions to neither.

No one ever sees it well,
not even a true believer.

Tocks

It is not then
or even likely now,
not any longer.

Tomorrow seems to
arrive before I
finish each today.

Time has no shortly
or just a bit more
but I wonder

is this phase I'm in
just some other thing
as I improve

or go under.

Vista II

The garage light glistens on
bastardized hurricane eddies —
rain *and* snow swirl in the air
this mid-December night.

Far from my Gulf shore,
New York wind and pines
mimic Indian Rocks surf
sounds during a storm.

Danger offers diverse
forms of death at nature's
hand. Cold steals dreams,
rocks you to a sleepy *finito*.

Gulf waters gain strength so
young surfers can confirm
bravado capacity to win or
lose in the game of life.

Watching from the porch,
nerves energized by the cold
raging howl, I thank small
gods for the passing vista.

Aries Horoscope: *The battles will be easier to fight when you think of them as being limited to today. Yesterday is gone and therefore is as uncontrollable as tomorrow. You will live triumphantly if you live in the present.*

Tomorrow's Yesterday

today I wonder

will tomorrow's yesterday

be win, lose, or draw

This is

The Next Part

Flop-a-ding-a-ly

Flop-a-ding-a-ly

the Monarch preps to fly south

I load the Buick

Countdown

Eight days left
until the flight,
a speck of time
or near eternity.
Man / Woman
Husband / Wife
House here
Condo there

Perhaps a
forward slash
is inappropriate.

Together.
Over fifty years
doing something
doing nothing
< the in between>
the out { } side

Countdown.
Asking.
What punctuation,
what symbol
fits these moments
or any?
Oh. Yes. That's IT!

∞

Identity II

Enter
without questions.
Silent

patiently
wait
listen.

You share
every name
given water.

Condo

this concrete beehive

buzzes away all day long

grows quiet at night

Van Goo

The bowl rests in the corner
on the counter near the sink,

a tomato and a lemon
close by.

The bowl holds apples,
bananas, oranges.

There will be no photo
or other oily work of art

for memory, only this
chuckling poet's mention

as I look toward some
fruit which may still join

the iced tea pitcher in the fridge
or a morning bowl of cereal

once one green, oozy, fuzzy
life form is removed from my

midst while I laugh here in an
un-artsy world of Van Goo.

another haiku

I started to say

but again interrupted

was about to say

Clearwater Sunset

He sat on the bench built into
the deck where it boxed out
larger than the rest of the pier.
Mom and dad stood at the railing
looking west. He sat in silence.

Short hair, tee, shorts, low-cut red Cons
and those cheap chrome aviators
every kid has owned or wanted.
Didn't need to see those eyes to
know he did not want to be there.

He was on the maybe side of
teenager. As the crowd grew
he seemed to shrink.
Sunsets always finish too soon.
"Jim come look! It's our last night."

Everyone heard it. "You see one
sunset, you've seen 'em all!"
I alone laughed, much too loudly
and walked toward the dimming
shoreline looking
for the ghost of Salvador Dali.

Florida

An afternoon
for a boy of six
measures three inches
of lizard.

Time in Out Time

On the porch before the sun rises, the vertical blinds still drawn but turned open to permit a view. The huge magnolia beyond the window forms a black suggestion of itself; a photo negative against the deepest murky-ness the sky can color just as the sun begins its work.

This is it.

My time in Out Time, when the world has yet to decide that specific grouping: the glorious moments when clocks seem slowed by the lack of light. When with vision dampened, my inner light graces thoughts held inside some boundary the world raises once a day.

Aloha

Out Time departing, the magnolia slowly becomes itself. Rhythms of the world expand in pulsations of light and sound like waves in our ocean of air until once again there can be time in Out Time. Pilgrimage ending, I worry into a dimmed window that has no reflection.

Groceries

She asks if I need anything
from the market across the street.
I check the pantry and say no.
She takes one of the store's carts
left in the hall & descends in the lift
as I watch her from the window.

I put Stevie Ray on the stereo,
sit down in the chair, back to the
window, tune up my black Les Paul.

It had been too long but I follow
the promise I made to myself over
twenty years ago, after the big one.

I can't ever be Stevie Ray but then
that was never the deal anyway and
I continue to improve as I go.

I lose myself in it. Then – yelling.
She's at the door. Groceries all over
the counters. The music still playing.

Bitter words follow. All because I did
not help as usual, did not see her return,
did not hear her at the door. Again.

The sadness hits me as it always will.
When it's Groceries — in the key of A.

Petition

My limitations —
stones on paths
I've yet to walk,

a small piece of paper
transformed to a bookmark
from a map never heeded.

***

The wind continues to
send our songs over roofs
at the top of the world.

My steps slowing,
I will burn the map piece,
pray the smoke finds you.

Somnolent

There it was
Again
After all this time
But how much
How long actually

One of *those*
The ones I hold as special
Magic words
Mouthwatering, akin to
a whole bag of Big-League

❖ ❖ ❖

Near dawn
I bring yesterday
to the back porch
Trade Minion jammies
for spattered blue jeans

Here it is
Again
Another day
kicking in
Always new
Beginning as I wonder
How long it will last

There is a Poem

There is a poem
     shaped like a bridge
          in Logan, Ohio.

It reads itself to us
     through a photo
          someone took,

a small arch type
     made from the stone
          it stretches above

in a glen.   Water flows down
     to unseen futures which
          Others may share

by looking at a photo
     or walking up to a bridge
          or reading a poem

that is a bridge
     to lead some of us
          toward Logan, Ohio

48

Aries Horoscope: *"You normally get where you want to go with a series of small steps, but not today."*

So — what should the title be? small steps
                    not today
                            getting somewhere
                                    getting anywhere

Not Today

Some of my grandsons' (Grant & Colin)
artwork greets my eye as I look around my
desk. Christmas is almost here and I will
see them later — but not today.

I thank the smaller gods for my life,
the incredible number of blessings
received as well as those to come
with each small step allowed.

The journey of each day brings me
new opportunities while I bounce
around on their roulette wheel of
my prospects.

I will use some to consider stories
by other hands.

Ballpark Wednesday

A ballpark Wednesday,

old friends gather in the sun.

Their twilight approaches.

With Old Friends II

A sunny day in early June
old friends gather at the ballpark.

Three stand waiting. A cell call.
One can't make it. They grumble
at the lost opportunity and go in.

The Mez is jammed with wheelchairs,
travel tempered by some of life's fires.

One of the three is fond of saying
Take it easy but *take* it and this,
unquestionably a day for it

the sights, sounds, smells as well
as the tastes — for taking it all in

the blessing for simply being alive
and best of all, a moment
with old friends.

"A bright but unsteady light has been awfully quenched." John Pendleton Kennedy's diary on Oct. 10, 1849, regarding the death of Edgar Allen Poe

Edgar

Love rose and fell for years
lingering and lurching to death.
He struggled for food
for shelter
for warmth from the cold
for the decency she so deserved
a safe place she could be held
and in the end, not hers but his —
they found him
lying on the street, possibly
in another man's clothes.

He dipped each pen
scratched each page
that we hold here
in our time
in our light —
as some of us might
try to reconcile his past
with now, to gather an
answer to questions
for how it all fits
or can't and never will.

Yet, still I stare
with all my might to see
back toward him.
To better understand
my own
unsteady light
and the flame
that remains
to be quenched,
awful
or otherwise.

A Bridge

M, Always
fch

A bridge
   in Patagonia
       stands above
          a stream,
surrounded by a forest
   with a single trail
       leading to a place
          I may never see
in person.
   Yet I have!
       A photo has led me
          and holds me there

nearly as tightly
   as you have
       for three score
          and more.

        ✿ ✿ ✿

And if I listen
   my intention grows
       with the sounds of
          a stream in Patagonia
and your heart here
   as it keeps time
       with mine
          along the path of
            our days;
       with steps to new bridges

Aries Horoscope: *"Agents of chaos keep group dynamics from getting stale."*

Agents of Chaos

The agents of Chaos
swim in the creek
near my ear
by my cheek

I blow my nose often
to stir up the air
keep them refreshed
and comfy in there

The old train trestle over Letchworth State Park gorge made so much noise that it drowned out the roar of the falls. Some daredevil teens, not to name names, were known to walk (or run) across the trestle.

Noise

Occasioned trains pass unheard
above the rumble of water
falling over ledges,
over stones in the path
below them.

Leaves rustle and grumble
to be heard as well as seen
on the breeze that passes
along the chasm on the way
to so many tomorrows.

Watch to see beyond
what is there with no sound
save your own heartbeat.
Savor it as the truth of noise
in the quiet of the universe.

In Your Company Again

My sight diminished

but delight never ending

Allowed to still watch

At Triphammer Falls

Torrents forces building upon each other
remain within their boundaries until fates
choices release them from gathering

So it is with these waters close by
So it is in the hills beyond the waters
So it is with their words

Floods carried trees to the log jam
in the stream where once, the Fates
allow some of us passage

When the torrents diminished, I returned
to the place under the bridge where
bones never buried sang ancient tomes

I stepped to the edge of the waterfall
as memories gathered and grew greater
I prayed the Fates allow me to remain

I waited a while to watch the mist in
the trees and listened to the roar
The words were sure to come

Eventuality

Eventuality hovers
at my shoulder
knowing full-well I
deserve to be convicted.

Regardless, I hand her
a book, ask that my
daughter read a
Jim Harrison poem.

My blood races faster as
her eyes roam the page.

Your young may arrive
at the courtroom rail
of your days as
prosecutor,
defender,
judge,
jury or
jailer.
Maybe even executioner...

But only for those
without poems.

A Kayapo Girl

My attention drawn to a mag
cover – the Amazon,
a young Kayapo girl
eyelashes and eyebrows
plucked clean, a small patch
of scalp shaved,
wide bright red stripes drop
from hairline past half the
eyes to each side of her nose.

One fine black line from
below the center of her
lower lip down her chin,
both cheeks patterned by the
same black lines outside the
lips all the way up to her ears.

But those eyes!
In each, tiny rectangles of
pure white light.

Probably nothing but physics of
background and camera,
yet it might better be considered
a light toward every
window of the world in all
our tomorrows.

The Glide

One re-reads Voltaire

the other Kesey's 'Notion.'

Futures posed as past.

Gravitas I

If only
    A portable gravity switch would be nice,
maybe built into my phone.

There is no wind at all this winter morning
but I am still unhappy.

A flip of the switch
and the flakes could fall so much slower.

One blue Sharpie diagonally across
a half dozen colored Brite Liners in the drawer,
lined up like sardines in a plastic tray,
phosphorescent blues, yellows, greens;
Varied collections — a blanket of desk clutter,
a miniaturization of my garage's grand scale.

If only life's inventory could be
counted as each slowed snowflake fell.

The value of it all summed to one smile,
a hug, a kiss for the equation's denominator

Packaged with heartfelt grace
for some future wind toward the next arrival.

The Speed of Time III

The sign out by the road warns
Speed Kills.
Inside, all our TVs loop a dawned
zurly light.
Cracked verticals speak a moist
blackness beyond
whispered apocrypha's plip-plop
tick-tock.

Questions stick to Mr. Crawdad's
infamy there
beneath stones the stream won't
surrender.
Rime builds a new shrouded
optical blend
acolytes use to choose up sides
for bankers.

Shops are selling a mutual
demurred destruction so we can
expect a banner year out here as
Speedo time
reaches past one second per sec
per dollar.
So,
go buy a new line Pilgrim —
I'll get us a revised script,
fresh bait and new poles
H-u-u-neee….

NIR

The letters stand for something:
No Imagination Required
I accept it, you may criticize me
after you finish reading this

If you are like me, a recent
development in science has
captured us all for good reason:
Nuclear fusion has happened.

The research has lasted for fifty-
plus years while the successful
experiment took less time than it
took a beam of light to move,

You ready?   One inch.

Why suggest no imagination
is required? Because you *must*
remain focused: you have lived
in every piece of that sort of time.

We are all riding the light that
travels anywhere, everywhere
light can go.

Deeper Motives

The old man spills some soup,
cusses at his clumsiness as he
reaches for some paper napkins.

Too near noon. The TV's running,
The Price is Right is nearly finished
but his mess demands more attention.

❊ ❊ ❊

Mess cleared; soup now consumed;
TV — a prosecutor explains charges
against two parents of a boy, fifteen.

Their teen son is accused of murder.
Four at school are dead and eleven
others remain hospitalized. For now.

❊ ❊ ❊

He points his clicker. TV is now off.
He feels welded to the kitchen chair
as his brain searches for a silence.

It keeps getting harder, finding quiet.
His mind roars with horrors visited;
war, a bugle's taps. Deeper motives.

❊ ❊ ❊

An old man doesn't need a TV. No.
Answers to questions? Elusive.
Silences between the two, worse.

66

Wander

I could die now
or see something new
Today
Or tomorrow
I'm not old

I could die now
Before I completed
apologies
After sorry
or Love You

Still

I could die now
or hear a new song
Today
Or tomorrow
I'm not deaf

I could die now
Before I taste them
Flavors
that remind me
of our lives or

I could live now
with your hand in mine
Wander
in each new next
piece of it

Still

Cornplanter's Shadow

A shadow passes unnoticed,
darker than death's night
across the first rays of dawn.

Cornplanter returns to the
sulfur spring east of the
Genesee river, across from
Canawagus,
his "Land of Stinky Water."

As a boy he enjoyed the cool
water still gurgling up to pool
there above mother earth.

The ancient river is tamed now.
Before, floods could hide the land
and this spring but only for a time.

Time.

He waits there by the spring to
reflect as he sings his song, one
only The People can know, that
no one can hear, the last song of
a sorrow that will go on and on
forever.

Witness

I listen while reading from our screened back porch. With the man door open, the garage radio blasts a song by The Doors and while the guitar break just after Morrison's singing "Well I did a little down about an hour ago" kicks in, a phantom sound that does not belong — a click begins to accompany the rhythm of the drum beats — not slightly mind you but exactly. I mark the page and rest the book on the table, listening more intently.

It continues with the song as my curiosity rises until I realize what the sound is; more a sort of blip than a click but a percussive element to be sure.

I had emptied the water from a bucket on the side of the house just around the corner from the porch to catch the water that drips from the small portable air conditioner in the family room window.

"city of night," blip "city of night," blip. I rise from the chair and walk outside to stand next to the bucket until the song is finished. I look to the sky and thank all the gods watching who allow my moment of witness. When it is over, I will go inside and break out my Les Paul.

Aries Horoscope: *"Your abiding respect for words and your love of their eloquent or novel expression will enhance your experience as you take part in a brilliant conversation or piece of writing."*

Both

Most "universal truths" have probably existed where they always were, smack dab center, so close to a middle that no science or even voodoo for that matter would ever define its location, between all the extremes that spread outward in all directions from that point, that exacting place nearly every one of us seems to lack a capacity to recognize.

Is it what the people we call genius are able to do? See with a vision we don't have the ability to shape, taste with tongues unlike our own, hear the music playing in spheres of influence way outside on the edges of paths as if they might be listening to buskers in some sort of space-time vortex beyond us all?

Is our depiction of a black hole not incorrect? Is it not linear? How many are there? How many today, next week, next however? Perhaps they have the capacity to redefine the meaning of Both . . .

Aztec Sunlight

The day's last sunlight

passing below the stone wall

whispers of Aztecs

Aries Horoscope: *"You'd love not to think of yourself at all – to be entirely unselfconsciously immersed in a state of flow as you execute the various activities of your day. Isn't that what true confidence is? You'll attain it for brief moments."*

Those Brief Moments

Call a few of them activities
Call some possibilities
Others atrocities

Call each of them an attainment
Upon some execution
The better ones

Mention all of the mid-fret shivers
Shrinking orbits of brevity
Other's druthers

In longest days or a dark just before
No truest confidence
can remain too long

until I hear John Hurt or someone
cut loose, then clocks stop
as I disappear

Fault Lines

Days become weighty choices
better left on the ground
along the fence line.

The afternoon sun slides away.

A breeze whispers secrets
in the pines of past
moments once shared.

Random firewood casually
stacked nearby waits patiently,
get-togethers now unlikely.

No fire songs or new memory
will light the dark again to lift
the weight of days.

The City of Angels

The citizens in the City of Angels
ran from streets paved with truth
for the sale of the century
at the megastore in
the City of Hype.

The medicine men traded their
golden wings for the dreams of
stacked profit margins at the
temple with the pulpit
of shattered glass.

They scratched their Psalms
on walls of ice that reached
the sky — where they went
to celebrate their
neighbor's woes.

It has always been so — where
ice falls into rivers carrying
the dust of the living
gliding along
with the dead.

This is

The Other

Part

Aries horoscope: *"Changing just one thing in a space changes the energy there. You'll use this to your advantage and affect the environment in interesting ways as you try to change the pattern there."*

Patterns

The words would not leave my thoughts,
Let's DO it! Let's do it right now!!
I did not understand the consequences.
Intended or otherwise, who does?

The day was already a doozy. Icy snow and
slush frozen an inch thick on
the car window. I needed to leave for the
airport soon. Since I could not get in the car to start
it, I began striking the windshield ice to
break it up.

After that bit of brilliance created a
pattern of cracks in the glass, I decided to
melt some ice with a torch. Much later I
boarded the plane hesitantly thinking,
My life has provided many patterns.

Vision Plus / Vision Minus

The eye surgeon says I'm OK
I need glasses but that's all
there is to it

I am relieved but don't tell him
what he has confirmed
Vision is a plus/minus deal

Now I *know* those things just
past my seeing are some ghosts
trying to convince me of things

Aries horoscope: *"Finding an answer will open the door for many new questions. For this reason, it is very important that you send your curiosity down the path you truly want to be involved with for the long haul."*

Pathways

I have thought about time since I was a child.
I'm an old man now, still thinking about time.
Trouble is, I'm running out of it. Day by day.
In this moment my thoughts have me feeling
like a copy of Crumb's Mr. Natural so I guess
I'll continue down my path and
Keep on Truckin'. . .

Thunder

Thunder overhead

lightning striking all around

I become smaller

The Last Question

A melody. Leon's 'Masquerade'. Now wafting toward his sunglasses and a potion for truth transferred from the bottle to his brain last night fixed it. His fortitude felt repaired. Was this somebody else's memory? A fortune teller mentioned a story written with two felt-tip markers on a deck covered with nutritional yeast and now, here he was. He stepped into the booth one roll of funky purple streamers circled the window.

"Fred, the name inside the band of Mr. Russell's top hat?"

"Al Jolson."

"Correct!"

Everyone cheered. The loudspeakers announced. "We now return to your regularly scheduled program. Embargo lifted."

Aries horoscope: *"It's not that you're shy. It's just that you don't always feel like talking to the others around you. Today's mood is unusual for you, but go for it. You'll appear mysterious and powerful."*

Powerful Mystery

It was a powerful mystery to him, for sure, that his
shyness could seem to make him appear
so mysterious and powerful.

Jack Elliot's Hat II

Jack Elliot's cowboy hat

is not *all hat and no cattle*

His jokes stay corralled

Share

Who defined insanity as doing the same thing over
and over while expecting a different outcome?

I forget; point is, if nobody seems to listen to you,
perhaps an unconventional audience will.

Don't forget to write the lines backward
and   sometimes well as left to right

Use an erasable pen on a big hand mirror.
Easy to replace one poem with the next.

Pick a sunny day and shine the words up
at the birds.

Don't waste your time with crows. They will not
wait to study what you had to say.

The blue jays will not only look patiently, they
squawk incessantly to anyone and anything.

They can be trusted
to share.

And always shine some words up into the cosmos.
Share Pilgrim, share.

Harvest

Wait. Moon tilts to peek
in the window, riveting and radiant
in this clear, dark, quiet, lonely moment
before dawn clangs announcements.

Fall only days away now.
Harvest time; gathering
summer memories for the
hearth that is a heart.

❋ ❋ ❋

Consider this season's lucre:
good health, two grandsons visit
with me in the pool, my reunion,
with a friend unseen for decades.

Snowflakes

huge snowflakes falling

the lawn with its next blanket

my thoughts travel south

What Matters

He told me he had cancer,
would be dead by October
but he made it to November,
then December and on into
the New Year.

When I saw him next, we
talked about a dream I had —
I was buying a life-sized
balloon of him, head to toe
wearing comfortable, colorful
clothes and even a really bright
red ball cap.

He began laughing his ass off.
As we sat there, he entertained
the idea more and more. I told
him I would try but my ability
to succeed was not good.

He remarked that the beauty of
the thought was enough, some-
thing we could both keep in our
thick skulls and he may leave me
behind but my thoughts — never!

3:47 a.m.

dense fog before dawn

hip pain stirring me from sleep

thankful for it all

Time & Tides

A foolish exercise
to be sure
Considering
me becoming me

It will undoubtedly
take longer
than I have

These fingerprints
still carry, still point
toward my tomorrows

Now & Then

The journal was on my knee
as unsteady as my hand.
The pen glided on its way
through plain moments.

This and that's filled in with
struggles tossing aside my
old fractions, parts of which
seemed to haunt, regardless.
* * *
Later I stepped outside,
looked up at the stars as I
recalled a lesson someone
shared long ago —

I am just a tiny portion of the
same matter which makes up
all those stars I see out there
in the night sky.

                    And more,
                    This pile
                    is conscious!

Another

Sunday dawns
another
Lanai coffee
another
Magazine
another
Short Story
another
Word Pile
another
Three Columns
another
Scene Set
another
Tale Unfolds
another
Not Mine
another
Shared Dawn
another
Day to
begin again

Back Scratcher

I open a drawer

for the bamboo back scratcher

a hand made by hand

A Senryu in Remembrance of Sam Cotter

Sam gave them a name

He referred to them as SWAs

suit-wearing a — holes.

Down to This

I sat reading outside on a languished afternoon
under a mall canopy away from the main entrance
in the smoking zone on a sparklingly clean poured
concrete bench near an ashtray full of butts as a man
approached from around the corner.

He was walking alongside a snazzy looking ten-
speed bike. He wore jeans, shiny black boots, a tee
shirt, sneaks, no beard and a haircut just around his
ears. He passed by without looking at me and stopped
at the other side of the entrance. I thought he was
looking for a bike rack to lock up the ten-speed so he
could go in and shop.

At the matching bench and ashtray he stopped,
turned and rummaged thru the cigarette butts.
He wasn't in any hurry and after stuffing some
in his pants pocket he came back my way. He
used the bike as a Viking might use a shield as a
barrier between us. He reached over it, sorted out a
few more cigarette butts and walked away toward
where he had come from.

I thought to myself — it's down to this.

I May Never

I may never learn —

The police took a homeless man away
some days after my call

    He has not returned
    It is unlikely he will

I sit looking out as the sun sets here in
that mystical time where transitions of
day to night can ask hard questions

    Who was he
    What more may be known

What of myself
Which of us is more
a missing person

    I may never learn —

Delicious

The flavor of pear,

pencil whispers on paper —

a delicious pair.

Dog Days

I am in two places at once.
I am in five times in two
places.

It is the locus point of our
entirety, where beginnings
bump into endings inside
infinite mixtures of space
and time itself here on this
tiniest blue-green grain of
sand on the shore of a sea
we call universe.

Our science may offer a
specific number of points
or places yet even here
the enormity of the total
stretches far beyond my
ability to grasp the whole.

I hear an LP's vinyl voices
singing how can you be
two places at once / when
you're not anywhere at all

Other Noises

I stand near the mailbox listening
as they pass by just above the trees.
Their wingbeats, brief whooshes.

They circle, descending cautiously
into the field across the road to rest
calling in another group to the west.

The paper tucked under my arm,
returning down the drive to the house —
my footsteps make no sound.

Waiting

I fold a paper napkin
in half
carefully placing it against
the small clock
next to the table lamp,

half the napkin flat
against the table,
the other half
upright,

covering the face
of the clock
as if time
had expired.

In the darkest hours
before dawn,
another journal
now filled;
the next,

blank with
a ribbon

Waiting.

A Poet's New Gauntlets

How might Seneca ghosts
view what may be perceived as
modern versions of gauntlets?

Jehovah's men wait at tables every
Friday outside the main entrance to
the public library.

He mumbles to *his* gods, evading
the warriors the best he can, quietly
chuckling to himself as he passes.

Girl scouts crowd his grocery doors at
Cookie Time — He smiles a No Thanks
while conjuring a Belushi movie scene.

Next time he is just as likely to think
of someone like a fellow poet —
albeit Charles Bukowski.

after

after a long life

building what you think you need

an end full of end

To Quotients

Joyce Carol Oates

I cringe at the intro praise
Not Again
Jesus H Christ

The woman is a word plague
A literature Barbie doll
Nearly every damn journal
I subscribe to, she's *there*
Sucking up space

My quotients
are out of whack
Leave poetry
For the rest of us
Would-ja Joyce

Three Amigos

Three amigos sat on a dock one summer night, a full moon shining down while smaller gods from worlds beyond them began the work of molding futures that were to follow.

Of course, none of us could have known that at the time. Andy and I were guitar troupers, already sorted away from big venues such as open mic nights at Gerde's Folk City. We soldiered on.

His cousin Jim had invited us to the cottage. Our lust for life was huge in those days. The small gods listened as we finished with *Gloria* by The Troggs. It was to be the last set we played together.

Unknown horrors stole Andy from us. Since then Jim and I have stepped from one path to another, Jim's as a successful author. I expect the small gods still have my list checked as TBD.

Jim and I still get together. An unplanned silence always occurs, regardless of the setting. One of us will look at the other and begin whispering.
G – L – O – R – I – A

Epilogue

Allow me this:

Rub your sounds for love
into my gravestone
with empty bare hands.

Return to your milieu.

Crumble this page.
Burn it. Make an
ink from the ash.

Write a message for
your tribe's generations
yet to be born.

Tell them of our days.

Notes

1. Foreword: With Jim Smith at his family compound.

2. Dedication: The Tanka is a 7th Cent. Japanese form originating prior to haiku. Originally 31 syllables with a 5/7/5/7/7-line pattern. Americanized versions often give up the strict 5 lines & 31 syllables. Mary is my reason for everything.

3. Page 8: An Americanized Haiku form; others can be found throughout.

4. Page 9: Homage to 23 Temple St. & sister Ann.

5. Page 10: Sisters Barb Davis & Steph Smith at cliff's edge above Canandaigua Lake. The camp inspires.

6. Page 12: Box lightning implies early Kodak cameras.

7. Page 14: I and many friends are still able to quote whole sections of skits by The Firesign Theatre.

8. Page 17: Our mother was a big-time naturalist.

9. Page 19: Titles help me organize my haiku work.

10. Page 27: I use 'scopes, by Holiday Mathis in the Democrat & Chronicle (Rochester, N.Y.), as exercise prompts.

11. Page 28: From a dream sequence.

12. Page 96: After Timothy Leo.

Acknowledgments

Sincere thanks to:

My wife Mary for every day I have been blessed to be in your company; daughter Libby and son Tom for their individual continual love and support; sister Ann Louise Driscoll for the guidance that brought me this far; James Herbert Smith, aka Smedley, for his wisdom and insistence; his wife Jacqueline (Rock Ledge Press), for her gentle command for the fruition of this work; and the entire Smith / Davis clan for the enrichment I continue to gain from time in their company.

Thanks to all my BBOMs and Sisters, Brian and Judy Reed, Dave and Anne Shanahan, John and Linda Mattie, the entire Mattie clan and Rocky Provencher — for without the strength of friendships like these a life jangles hollow, the music out of tune. That just ain't no darn good whatsoever.

Big Love!
fcb

About the Author

Fred Harrington and his wife Mary have been friends with Jim Smith since they were students at SUNY Brockport. The Harringtons now divide their time between a condo near Florida's Gulf Coast close to Indian Rocks Beach and their farmhouse built in the 1800s south of Lake Ontario, between Rochester and Buffalo, New York.

Printed in the USA
CPSIA information can be obtained
at www.ICGtesting.com
JSHW020721070823
46061JS00003B/186